Ali Cobby Eckermann | Inside My Mother

Kat sweetheart,
I love you very much,
Rouise
x x x x x
december '17

New Poems

GIRAMONDO POETS

Ali Cobby Eckermann | Inside My Mother

First published 2015
from the Writing & Society Research Centre
at the University of Western Sydney
by the Giramondo Publishing Company
PO Box 752 Artarmon NSW 1570 Australia
www.giramondopublishing.com

Designed by Harry Williamson
Typeset by Andrew Davies
in 10/16.5 pt Baskerville

Printed and bound by Ligare
Distributed in Australia by NewSouth Books

National Library of Australia
Cataloguing-in-Publication data:

Eckermann, Ali Cobby
Inside my mother / Ali Cobby Eckermann

ISBN 9781922146885 (pbk)

A821.4

This book is dedicated to my mothers
Mum Audrey Ngingali, Aunty Mabel,
Aunty Lorna, Aunty Lola, Aunty Nura,
who in their passing strengthened me
to know who I am

and to

Mum Frieda and Mum Jennifer
who still remain
my dearest friends

and to my special 'bonus daughter'
from your 'bonus mum' with all my love

Other books by Ali Cobby Eckermann

Little Bit Long Time
Kami
His Father's Eyes
Ruby Moonlight
Love Dreaming and Other Poems
Too Afraid to Cry

Acknowledgements

Many thanks to my family for their support while I wrote this collection, especially my sisters in Port Pirie, Annette, Judith, Allison and Lena, brother Christopher, Aunty Raelene Wingfield, cousin Rosina and friends Samia Khutan, Mandy Brown, Michelle Leber and Lionel Fogarty. I also thank the many poetry friends who cared for me during my overseas travel, including Bernice Chauley (Malaysia), Lee Martin and family, Quaisra Shahraz, Holly Ringland and Sam Harris, Chiew-Siah Tei, Maggie Gibson, Anita Scott (UK), the entire IWP14 family at the University of Iowa, Valencia, Andrea Wilson and Bob Holman (USA). Special thanks to Mridula Chakraborty, Seemantini Gupta, Ananya Dutta Gupta and the many friends at Jadavpur University Kolkata, who always give much joy.

This project has been assisted by the Commonwealth Government through the Australia Council, its arts funding and advisory body.

Contents 1

2

3

4

1

Bird Song

our birds fly
    on elongated wings
        they fly forever
            they are our Spirit

           our bird song
        is so ancient
    we gifted it
to the church

Australantis

there's a whole ocean filled with sand
between what was and what will be

where fish grow wings to climb the sky
and water birds revert to earth

a stark canvas devoid of view
not a sand dune nor a tree

only a shell hangs beyond the skyline
spilling the noise of the in-between

Tjukurrpa

for Aunty Phyllis and Aunty Eileen RIP

tribes gather on the sand
at the ancient birthing place

a magic pelican child is born
a carry basket is woven from reeds

baskets are woven with story
baskets are woven with song

my basket is heavy with history
out of sight like superstition

our footsteps in the sand
will turn to rock soon

my father is the sand dune
that rock is my mother

Love

there is love
in the wind by
the singing rock

down the river
by the ancient tree
love in malu

ngintaka and kalaya
love when spirits speak
no human voice

at the sacred sites
when walawaru soars
over hidden kapi

find the love

Kulila

sit down sorry camp
might be one week might
be long long time

tell every little story
when the people was alive
tell every little story more

don't forget 'em story
night time tell 'em to the kids
keep every story live

don't change 'em story
tell 'em straight out story
only one way story

all around 'em story
every place we been
every place killing place

sit down here real quiet way
you can hear 'em crying
all them massacre mobs

sit down here real quiet
you can feel 'em dying
all them massacre mobs

hearts can't make it up
when you feel the story
you know it's true

tell every little story
when the people was alive
tell every little story more

might be one week now
might be long long time
sit down sorry camp

Owls

in stillness I lay
hours before the dawn

an owl wakens me
from slumber

kuur kuur
kuur kurr

in softness I lay
listening to its call

kurr kurr
kurr kurr

in calmness I lay
to empty my mind

is it a message or
simply a song

kuur kuur
kuur kuur

Trance

1

an old woman's eyes mist over
ghost gums begin to dance
fire light flickers
the night air prepares its exit

hunched in her possum skin cloak
the dawn breeze chills
a whisper inside her trance
the sound of instinct

2

in her mind she observes both
the hardness of the trunks
and the softness of bark
and requires neither

she floats in a pituri haze
among the river of trees
bleached sand burns her skin
she enjoys the sensation

heat is the love of the campfire
the yellow kiss of the sun
the passion that flows after hunting
and life, before her man died

in her trance she observes
the hard and the soft of trees
branches uplift his bark-bound body
there is no request more sacred

heat was a grip with fingers entwined
the firmness of his torso
the instrument of his voice
his smile missing in her empty hand

Abstract

she remains beyond her imagination
no imprints mar her mind

its undulating discourse informs a briny view
large fish bones lie scattered on moist sand

a thin track cuts to the matrix below
the illusion of turquoise is scented with birth

the sea water spills a treasure of shells
at her feet the murmur of legends crave her

one foot in water, one foot on sand
the tidal gravity keeps her grounded

rough-and-ready art erupts from her
she breathes air into a dead gull

sticking feathers in her eyes
she has resigned the human realm

she scribes patterns into her mind
and naked she executes her future

Canoe

a girl watches a bead of sweat roll
tracing the muscles on his arms
as he lowers the freshly cut bark
moist grass provides a cushion

he turns to stare at her stillness
her eyes remain above his head
the soft flesh of the tree expires
the scar bleeds on the trunk

outside the smoky fire she stands
he dries and shapes the fresh canoe
the structure forms to natures laws
a new dais of voyage prepared

at midnight they sail the river
she turns without causing a ripple
looking back along the darkness
to the neon of the scar tree

it shines like a bended doorway
a light within beckons as if a
sacred star has fallen and a
yearning will soon be done

Seeds

there are always seeds that thread us
and carried on the wind set us apart

does the wind come from the origins
of the mother or the father

will my origins be blown away
or remain in distance if I leave

will the wind stand breathless
shall I remain to die broken from home

Ooldea Soakage

the big sand hill is
smaller now reduced
in the memory of
my mother

digging down into
the waterhole no
water remains for
the dingoes

overhead the sky
continues to shine
mother and daughter
standing together

at the tribal camp
we gather old coals
history trapped inside
rubbing charcoal on skin

Amnesia

when I open my eyes
I do not remember who I am
a girl is teasing me so I chase her
I cannot conceive she is my daughter

in the village I beg *do you know me*
as paupers fling crumbs at my feet
the street grows narrower
silent dogs trail behind me

Heartbeat

boobook owls permeate
their call transmutes me

I cannot see this orchestra
only the sky beyond the trees

my ears adjust to flicks of light
a miasma of dark and afar

my heart retains the singing
the story a language

the song of owls pulsates
as trees guard the sky

Innermost

her husband was killed in a hunt
they had only been married three moons

she sits inside a treeless forest
deep within sorry business

when blue skies appear she asks for dusk
when she sees clouds she prays for stars

all stays the same the sun the night
nature does not change for her requests

Clay

the world is turning to clay
its muddy weight dry on my skin
drags me down below river banks
reducing the sky to a sliver

all peripheral vision is blocked by earth
the sky allows a sight that does not end
only my eyes reveal the myopia secret
my desire to live in the sky

the sky remains free from blemish
the depth of this view reduces me
shrinking me back into the earth
only the whites of my eyes suggest clouds

the clay on my skin has dried and cracks
its earth voice hoarse, now drowned in mud
I retreat to myself encased in knowing
truth is bigger when reduced in size

Inside My Mother

my mother screams as I touch her hair
attempting to brush away the coarseness with my hands
to entwine twigs full with leaves into her locks
a tiara of green to soften her face
and our tears dry now my mother is frailing
she talks only to those who have gone before
no longer seeing my love, no longer needing

and the wailing bursts from our mouths
as she sinks to the ground, her mother the earth
my mother the dying
throws sand in her face, tasting the grit
in her mouth and wailing louder throws herself
forward, pushing her breasts into the softness
of the earth her mother and
my mother the dying

crawls down into that final embrace
her conversation incoherent now
as if like a child she is practising words
for the lifetime to come
and the syllables loud and guttural spill
over the sand her mother the earth
and I walk away leaving her there

in that cradle, safely nestled in the roots
of that tree, safe in her country
our solace her grave

Dip

my mother is playing hide and seek
between my memory and my dreams

she hides amongst the Language Speakers
I catch glimpses of her laughing

no longer foetal I must arise
no longer prone she has arisen

I see a foot dip daintily
In a rivulet of fresh rain

Is it hers or is it mine?

Shadows

silhouettes of birds flit across a purple sky
the outline of their shapes stir an old memory

bird shadows fall to the earth around me
like a slide show of family memorabilia

wherever their shadow hits the ground a tree grows
I stand inside a forest and can no longer see the sky

Lament

I can not stop
must sing my song

I can not stop
must sing my song

the old man chants
his boomerangs ring

I am the last speaker
of my mother tongue

I   can not   stop
must   sing   my   song

my   song   must   not
die before   me

2

The Gunbarrel Highway

it is an unknown to walk through drought
urged by the rumour of rations and a
readiness to beg for water

it is an unknown for mouths to blister
forced to suckle from the white man's hand
and bear his children

it is an unknown to be fed a famine
forced separation between parent and child
every stomach is empty now

the unknown legacy is to beg forever
coerced by the fallacy of endless promise
and cups of poisoned water

Mamu

1

the first metaphor is a dead bird
I have murdered it

and the glee that fills me
is like sugar

when I ice the cake
to celebrate days of death

I hang lanterns
from my eyes

2

the skull of a catfish
is trapped in mud
its eternal grin
its naked sharp teeth

a cragged rosary
is set in its jaw
where once the tongue
now a toad is there

the squish of raw mud
as I pluck the skull
is an echo of intimacy
aloof from conscience

Shells

in an aisle
of middens he
blocks her advance

his shiny shell
embellished spear in
hand

watching her
paint her body
white ochre

her breasts
her stomach her
thighs

glisten white on
alabaster skin

soon to turn
red

Clapsticks

clapsticks ring syllables of song
the song lives in the eagle flying overhead
watch for the glint of light from its wing
as it turns in tune with the sun

do not flinch away from angels
they come to appraise the song
in the amphitheatres of our mouths
and the inflation of our hearts

the rightful season is now
sing your love toward the sky
play them clapsticks my sister
the song exists in your heart

Kumerangke

she wakes upside down
the ground is ocean blue

dried blood sticks her head down
she stares at an orange sky

clouds of kangaroos bound
rapid on the horizon

a loving culture ricochets
thunder rocks in nearby hills

campfires are lit along coastlines
spears are lined behind the dunes

clutch the nulla nullas
eagle sits with kangaroo

rattle the boomerangs
cockatoo sits with dingo

in the sliver between terrain and tomb
she watches silent bones drift skyward

Warriors At Salt Creek

A tribute to the fierce warriors Moorcangua and Mongarawatta, of the Milmenura people, who fought the dispossession of their land along the Coorong 1830–1841

Why are our modern day
warriors hanging from trees?

As they circle the sun
tides agitate the sand dunes

As muted tongues swell
hatchlings shriek from grassy knolls

Crows gather and walk the sand
This vision can never leave their eyes

As the warriors circle the sun
Will footprints gather in their shadows?

As they circle the moon
Are we free to cut them free?

The creak of the rope is intrusive
The howl of the wind is a knife

Why are our modern day warriors
hanging from trees?

Rust

we walk to the river
dying slowly

there is no one to meet us
by the circle trees

we watch canoe trees
turn to ghosts

as the water vanishes
to rust we wonder

will the Serpent lose its rainbow
if the river runs dry?

Vengeance

Kadaicha I whisper
a single bird call tells
he is near

Kadaicha I whisper
a single bird call tells
he is kin

Kadaicha I whisper
a single feather tells
he is here

Summer

a tree explodes
a shatter of splinters
in a summer storm

every sliver transforms
into a bird shape
countless will remain

in feather country
dancing is endless to
the music of wood

Unearth

let's dig up the soil and excavate the past
breathe life into the bodies of our ancestors
when movement stirs their bones
boomerangs will rattle in unison

it is not the noise of the poinciana
stirred by wind in its flaming limbs
the sound of the rising warriors echo
a people suppressed by dread

a hot wind whips up dust storms
we glimpse warriors in the mirage
in the future the petition will be everlasting
even when the language is changed

boomerang bones will return to memory
excavation holes are dug in our minds
the constant loss of breath is the legacy
there is blood on the truth

Kaleidoscope

a boy sits on the shore of languages, water babbles
there are no rocks, no constants, the tide laps gently

on the horizon sunset appears and colours stretch
twilight will arrive like vowels that sustain the sky

stars burst in a global dance, in the distance a didgeridoo blows
comets script the language names, the boy recognises his own

the sea babbles and blurs, the ocean becomes a kaleidoscope
agitating nightfall into shards that cling and separate

starlight refracts for a moment swirling its message
the boy lays down on the shore for a better view

the kaleidoscope begins to turn a little faster
the language names are twining like invisible string

the shards pirouette and fall upon each other
and the boy is sated, waiting for the approach of new

Footprint

the moment you jumped from your boat
and landed on the shore
your footprint stood next to mine

in the morning my footprint had disappeared
and yours remained
it would not leave

the incoming tide betrayed me
wallowing in water I am drowning
I spy my footprint on the moon

the reflection on the shore is boundless
like a warrior sure under the moons glow
your footprint trapped now in a shallow pool

Sadness

I have become allergic to
your Sadness yet you remain
relentless seeking me out
embarrassing us both with
your Sadness carrying it
around clinging to it for grim
life until your Sadness
sprouts from you like tendrils
binding my feet that once
were free

Hindmarsh Island

cars drive over the babies
no one cares at the café
it's a lonely place for pelicans
now the fish are polluted

it's a troubled bridge over water
only our tears fill the river
its mouth filled with screaming sand
Aunty hold my mullaway hand

sing the pelican song
sing the blue sky refrain
it's a troubled bridge over water
the signs are posted at Signal Point

Oombulgarri

tumble weeds of blue pattern dresses
drift down empty streets
where paddy wagons once patrolled

the town is empty now
as empty as the promises
that once held it together

even the wind can no longer stir
movement at the playground
all the equipment is rusted shut

echoes of laughter roll like distant thunder
but unlike a storm cannot pass by
hysterical energy whips and wails, and wails

tumble weeds form an interwoven frenzy
a fortress to guard the perimeter of this site
broken, even the creak of the gate is silent

Eyes

her eyes stare to challenge her
from a plate on the kitchen table
which eyes will she need for today?

the eyes of terror she has thrown away
the eyes of submission are blinded now
she avoids the eyes of shame

her hand hovers above the plate
will she choose eyes of wonder or contempt
will she choose eyes full of compassion

the eyes are watching her eyes
that can soothe or sting her tears
she picks the eyes filled with rage

Lake Eyre

we float our churches down the river
      and you will not know
you do not see our religion

the reeds will share our journey
      weaving and weaving our songs
into objects of splendidness

on every river bank we embark
      a ceremony will be sung
a sacred ritual of love

the warriors will comfort the sick
      near journeys end
the lame will walk to join the dance

we will build a synagogue at Kati Thanda
      multitudes of birds the choir
the feathers stretched in praise

A Cross

the bullet has left your pistol
it has not reached the target of my chest

the air burns between you and me
I hold my breath for the irretrievable impact

in the eternity of a generation
I stare at the void between us

I throw my arms out to the sky
my shadow stark as a wooden cross

3

Tjulpu

life is extinct without
bird song

dream birds arrive
at dawn

message birds tap
at windows

guardian birds circle
the sky

watcher birds sit
nearby

fill my ears with
bird song

I will survive

Love 22/06/10

I want to climb inside you
transfuse your heart blood to mine
of course that cannot happen

we can link in other ways
when your hands search
for mine at night time

inside your arms there is peace
a timelessness I have not known
were we lovers in the Dreamtime?

First Born

I want to hold my son
like a new born babe

reassure my son that
my hold is forever

but he is gone
or is it me?

the air feels cold
where once you lay

and where I sit
an empty place

Gunfire In Spring

it is the thirst for equality
that both unites and destroys
our minds like gunfire in spring

you are the heirs of kings and I
I have risen from your garden
seeking knowledge, yes

we share this but you are
the conquerors and I
I refuse to be conquered

the stalks of flowers point skyward
long after the bullets have struck
the petals sigh back into the earth

I Tell You True

I can't stop drinking I tell you true
Since I watched my daughter perish
She burnt to death inside a car
I lost what I most cherished
I seen the angels hold her
As I screamed with useless hope
I can't stop drinking I tell you true
It's the only way I cope

I can't stop drinking I tell you true
Since I found my sister dead
She hung herself to stop the rapes
I found her in the shed
That rapist bastard still lives here
Unpunished in this town
I can't stop drinking I tell you true
Since I cut her down

I can't stop drinking I tell you true
Since my mother passed away
They found her battered down the creek
I miss her more each day
My family blamed me for her death
Their words have made me wild
I can't stop drinking I tell you true
'Cos I was just a child

So if you see some one like me

Who's drunk and loud and cursing

Don't judge too hard 'cos you don't know

What sorrows we are nursing

Full Moon

at midnight thoughts of you infiltrate
my mind. it is the sound of chains
sliding across a cold stone floor

an old man sways from the ceiling
mocking me. the sound of chains is softer
than the creaking of rope

his image is louder in darkness
I dare not shut my eyes
is there a lullaby to quell the dead

we share each full moon together
old man did I know you do you know me
 the tension inside this room is not a lullaby

outside the arms of boab trees
scratch against the moon
it is no longer yellow

Cross Road

every morning when he departs her bed
she promises *I will never marry you!*

his inside face hides from public scrutiny
in the wardrobe with silverfish and mice

the cat on the windowsill hisses every time
his outside face appears at the window

scurry before the tears of despair fall
build a wooden heart, not a spear

slaughter emotions one by one till
the coolamon is filled with blood

when the suffering has dried
grasp the spearing barbs of misery

plunge away from memory
walk naked to the grave

on the windowsill the cat hisses
staring with crossroad eyes

Monsoon

He's crawling through the long grass
Like condensation sliding down a tower
    His tongue swollen from dehydration

Despite drenching rains his skin is hot
The monsoons torture his poverty
    A lifestyle that eats from the inside out

At the squalid camp the cooking fire still burns
Tendrils of smoke drift between raindrops
    As rainbows dance on pandanus leaves

He crawls into his sodden bed
The blankets slowly rotting around his flesh
    As prisms catch on rain washed leaves

Paradise remains here despite the mess
Renewal arrives as sunshine breaks free
    From low grey clouds that often moan

Friendship arrives in a shopping trolley
The wheels mark a double highway to the shops
    Gratitude mutes the monsoon mayhem

Marry Up

sit down
chuck in
yarn up pass
out

pretty woman sit
down centrelink
queen chuck in
yarn up pass out
you love me hey
pretty woman sit
down chuck in you
drink 'em mine
yarn up pass out
you marry me hey

sit down long time
chuck in all you got
yarn up stick fight pass
out pass away

The Letter

Dear Mother
The mission is good.
The food is good.
I am good.

rips the page from the typewriter
scrunches the page till it bleeds
kicks it under the wardrobe

inserts a fresh page
tentatively with finger
poised and types

Mummy
Where are you?

Rites

in the dormitory
we cut our arms

fill the gashes with ash
from the dirty hearth

one girl gets infected
the doctor cuts her arm off

the remainder of us
admire our scars

the notch of grief
a cultural rite

Leaves

that lone tree on the ridge
is that my father?
it stands like him

in my mind the horizon is
formed by him even at this
distance I know that

grass plains sway to sweep
the void there is no chasm
between us

I crawled there once and sat
in his shade he did not know me
yet gave me leaves

now only a few leaves
remain on ageing limbs
to beckon his story

if I climb to him now
and lie in his limbs
will our story unite?

will the leaves turn golden
and seeding grass sway
to console me?

Severance

as the spinifex touch
of your mothers' hand

                                    is

                                    severed

from the sand hill
of your cheek

a baby's cry

                                    lingers

    framed
   in   an
empty window

when your own born child
    gets
    whisked
              away
                        from
o u t s t r e t c h e d   longing

                                        sky
                              the
                         to
                    smoke
               of
          tendril
like a

if you can't trust the womb

how can you trust the universe?

Fear

she wakes
smelling dogs on
the horizon

fear permeates
from her essence as
a woman

the dogs bark
their mouths a sin
she cannot escape

she tastes the saliva
from devouring maws
blood starts to flow

the essence of her
remains trampled in
a bloody pool

A Promise

She gives him a cloud of parrots
He expects her to peel the carrots
She gives him a safari cruise
He expects her to hide the bruise
She gives him a blue magic rabbit
He expects her to feed his habit

He gives her a kicking horse
She expects his true remorse
He gives her a milking cow
She expects his help somehow
He gives her his silver spoon
She expects she'll kill him soon

Pira

we are penniless
muffled in low light
the moon chuckles

here is the moon
that has robbed us
of foresight

we hide from its grin
as curiosity extends
its eye to find us

under a shroud
we have stolen
back the cynicism

Ngingali

my mother is a granite boulder
I can no longer climb nor walk
around

her weight is a constant reminder
of myself
I sit in her shadow

gulls nestle in her eyes
their shadows her epitaph
I carry

a pebble of her in my pocket

4

Key

a girl stands outside Grandmothers door
it is painted blue with a speck of gold
she stares and squints her eyes a little

there is a gap along the bottom
a stretched and lipless grimace
that breathes in and out and in and out

some days the respiring air stinks
footsteps stumble and scuffle the floor
her ears strain to catch a muffled whisper

sunlight through the hallway window
marks the spot where she stands
on the rim where light and shadow meet

sometimes she smells the faint hint of smoke
hears the slight crackling of fire
on those days she hears laughter

sometimes she recognises the fragrance
of storms approaching and stands transfixed
watching water trickle past her toes

Grandmother never invites her inside the room
the creak of bedsprings heralds her exit
the little girl never stays to pry

unconditionally she waits down the hallway
on exit Grandmothers hand always reaches for hers
in the kitchen Nana cheers her with biscuits

their time is sparse like a dying tree
neither glance at the keyless door
nor expect more from each other

a girl and her grandmother sit in contrast
two kindred spirits swaying their feet
as if in rhythm to an unknown tune

the girl stands at Grandmothers door
there is no key hole to the future
and no vision to the past

Mining

Grand daughter wants her to drive slowly
So she can count the white posts along the highway

56...57...58...59 and oh Nana
You're driving too fast Nana!

Nana keeps her eyes on the road ahead
Checks the rear view mirror for mining trucks

22...23...24...25 slow down Nana
I can't count that fast!

The old woman smiles at her grand daughter
The young girl smiles at her Nana

A truck slams in to the slow moving car
They count as road toll now

A Tragedy

a joey fell out of its pouch and rolled,
stopping at my feet twigs and dirt and
ants camouflaged its beauty holding it
against my chest our heart beats touch without
turning my head I know the
mother is watching from the sand hill
despite the fact her carcass lays dead
on the roadside before us the joey's
eyes meet mine there is trust in tragedy

Sacrifice

she brought her daughter
to the feet of the man
who sits on the mountain

once there she crumbles
her need of him is greater
she strips bare her beauty

the man on the mountain sits
like a rock, eyes unmoving on a
horizon shimmering with lust

the sobs of the daughter muffle
the sobbing of the mother and
at night become one

Legacy

await in the space of
your heart that
cannot be filled

await for the words of
promise that turns
feathers into swords

await for the touch
of trust to stroke and
stab your thighs

wait for the hug of warmth
the comfort that imprisons
with embroidered handcuffs

await in the space
of your heart that
cannot be filled

Eve

oh that vulnerable girl
she had such a temper
storming off to the coast
before learning to fish

now she's angry and hungry
marching off to the city
to beg for food

in her innocence she
covets the greedy people
who have more than she

a butterfly flits to her
transforming the urge
greed is insatiable

Heat

the wind is hot and smells like snakes
a young man sits in the shade of a cliff

he is carving a story in the rock with chisel
and hammer he stole from the store

sweat covers his body and burns his eyes
he is relentless in his task

even the wind seeks respite in the shade
as if observing the composition of his work

it is a story of creation
it is the story of the snake man

it is a story gifted in his dreams
now realised in the physical

on completion he whispers *liru*
then lowers his tools and walks away

the wind is hot and smells like snakes
heat will not obliterate legend

Believe

the boy walks with a noose
around his neck the end frays
where it touches the ground

no-one teases him on these days
no-one wants the blame for
any potential consequence

he wanders the streets
peering in windows
as people scuttle for their safety

the bottle shop lady is beautiful
her reflection caught his attention
through frosted glass doors

giddy up she laughs
as she leads him home
he feels giddy!

they unravel the noose
weaving a carpet
for their future

sometimes visitors catch
the word BELIEVE as
they wipe their feet

Jacob

she grew so tired
listening to his requests
any cough lolly? where's
the smokes? waru?
where's the waru?

where's my puffer? you seen
my Archie Roach cd? where's
the remote control?

where's the car keys? you
seen my wallet? where's
my hat?

every time he leaves the house
or at night when he sleeps
she hand sews his new coat
with many pockets

she fills the pockets
with cigarettes and lighters
his necessary credentials
his medical supplies

with weary eyes she smiles
handing the new coat to him
smiling he bit her for fifty
then headed for the casino

in the morning he says
stay in bed dear
you rest now
I'll make breakfast

there's no food in the fridge
he's gotta go to the shops
he's looking for his wallet
gently he asks her
you seen my new coat?

Please Brother!

as the plane began to descend
she asks him *bruz ya want some*
water (to swallow) *for your ears*

yeah he says holding
the bottle how much
do I put in?

Nurture

she never received enough nurturing
before she become the nurturer

hanging out load after load of washing
for those who lay sleeping on the couch

washing and drying dishes each day
while others hurled plates at each other

babysitting the children when they went to score (drugs)
pretending it was a date night for Indian curry

she carries her grandson in the wheelbarrow
teaching him about the wind, and the sky

they collect firewood for the campfire
when he sleeps she sits alone staring into the flames

she longs for some nurturing from the Old People
her mother's breath on her cheeks

a gentle hand at her elbow
the peaceful kiss of night

A Rose

it was such a blessing
the beauty of an exquisite rose
a single flower

obsessed she insists
mass planting in the garden
the bouquet overpowering

now beauty is a chore
and the blessing
forgotten

A Handful Of Weeds

a woman lays down in the grass
squints one eye against the sky
changing grass stalks to towers of gold

her grandson lays beside her
telling stories of malu and tjulpu
he imitates their movements
in that old sacred dance

a blue-tongue lizard lumbers past
its tongue protrudes from pinkness
its mouth surreal and hissing

the boy is surreal in his love of her
the patter of his feet is her pulse
his skin shines with his trust of her

at dusk headlights force a crusade
in the moment before discovery
he puts a handful of weeds on her grave

My Mission

Yesterday

I ate fresh oysters with
my mother sitting at
her grave

we tied plastic flowers onto
her wooden cross under a
blue sky

Today

I will visit family
who my mother knew before
she was stolen

we will sit at the mission making
damper together sharing
kangaroo tales

Strings

in her hands she holds the
strings attached to the
generations each side of her
a sharp wind stirs the strings
cutting her hands
slicing her palms and despite the pull
her feet refuse to budge or
leave the ground

Today

today I found the tree under
which my mother was born
her placenta was buried here
as her ashes are now

today I found a broken toy
its wooden arms removed by time
framed by footprints that may lead
to kangaroo men on the horizon

today I found a broken house
its window blank and mouth askew
yet in the tangled rusty mess
gems of sentiment lingered

today I became a weeping tree
a vision of memory deep inside
a face embedded in its bark
the mirror of my mum

Lyre Birds

meet me at the river
where lyre birds hide
    maybe
we will catch a glimpse of them
        maybe

hold me in that place where
shyness and lyre birds meet
    maybe
the tangle of thorns will retreat
        maybe

touch me softly oh so softly
stroke feathers on my cheek
    maybe
my softness will return
        maybe

The Last Cuppa

and she just knew that one day she
would fall asleep under the blanket
that she carried everywhere as a veil
from the evils of the world

and she just knew that the blanket
would be decorated with a lap rug
that her son had tucked around her so
he could hold her one last time

and she just knew that her daughter
would just know when to come to
dislodge the cup of tea grown cold
from the stiffening of her fingers

and brush her hair

Evacuate

today I will relinquish
my body

I shall process my
dreams of tragedy

my eyelids flicker
as I wait for eagle

only then can I
return to myself